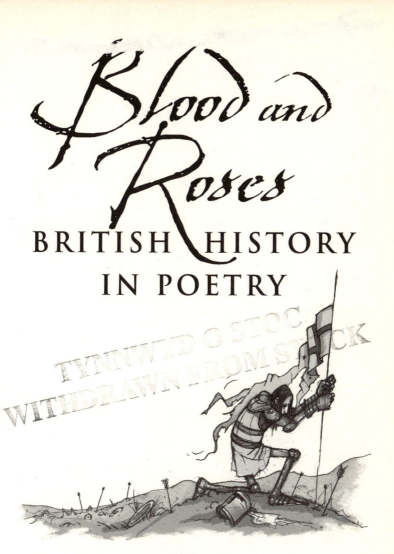

Blood and Roses

BRITISH HISTORY
IN POETRY

Compiled by BRIAN MOSES

Editor: Katie Orchard
Designer: Jane Hawkins

Published in Great Britain in 2004 by Hodder Wayland

This paperback edition published in 2005 by Hodder Children's Books

Cataloguing in Publication Data
Moses, Brian, 1950–
  Blood and Roses: British History in Poetry. – (Poetry Powerhouse)
  1. Great Britain – History – Juvenile poetry
  I. Title
  821.9'14

ISBN: 0 3408 9388 5

Printed and bound in Great Britain by Clays Ltd,
St Ives plc, Bungay, Suffolk

The paper and board used in this paperback by Hodder Children's
Books are natural recyclable products made from wood grown in
sustainable forests. The manufacturing processes conform to the
environmental regulations of the country of origin.

Hodder Children's Books
A division of Hodder Headline Limited
338 Euston Road, London NW1 3BH

Introduction

History is about connections. Connections between the past and the present. It is a journey between what we were and what we have become, offering up clues that allow us to see ourselves on the different stages of that journey.

A chronological perspective is important when we take an overview of history and this consideration has led me to arrange these poems in order of time and subject matter. Our journey begins with the Stone Age and the flint that is buried in the earth, only to be discovered centuries later. It ends with the recent troubles in Northern Ireland, events which themselves have roots stretching way back in history.

I have tried to include a mixture of poems. Some will be familiar chestnuts, old friends of the poetry world that we feel comfortable with. Others have a bit of an edge, which may lead us to question what we thought we knew about an historical event. Some may hold surprises. Some of the contributors will be familiar names, but there are new names here, too.

Although this is a history of Britain, it is important to remember that our country did not become what it is in isolation, and many of the poems reflect this view. History, too, is not just about kings and queens, and again I have tried to steer clear of too many poems that merely describe our monarchs. I preferred, instead, to include poems that give us a taste of the times (and an aroma, too, as in *Bess's Bath*).

So, come travel in time with me, and I hope that you enjoy reading this collection as much as I have enjoyed making the selection.

Brian Moses

Contents

The Flint

Who lived in these ancient woods?
Many thousands of years ago
small men made their dwellings here –
lugged the great stones to and fro
and beneath a sheltering bough
ate, and slept, as I do now.

Who last held this flint? I guess
someone sharpened it to be
a precious weapon ... kept it safe...
used it often, skilfully,
carved an arrowhead, and slit
the creature's throat he slew with it.

Who felt spirits in the trees?
Saw the sun rise like a god
on its journey east to west?
Who sniffed water, understood
where it wandered through the ground
and marked the spot it might be found?

Who walked on this ancient track?
Short and muscular, he wore
skins to cover him, and lit
fires to warm the winter's core.
In my hand (how strange it is!)
I hold the flint he held in his.

Jean Kenward

Silent Stones

Standing stones and circles,
Circles, standing stones
Never tell as much as trinkets,
Pots and crumbling bones.

Yes, we know who built them,
Yes, we've tried and think
This is how they did it,
And how long ago – *we think*.

But it's all just guesses, guesses.
Stones are stones, with voiceless throats,
Masterminds at keeping secrets
From a time when no one wrote.

Why they built them?
How they used them?
Things we'll never really know.
Still we come
    to see
    to touch.
Still the mystery grows.

It's the mystery of not knowing.
It's far more than what stones show.
It's the mystery of feeling
How we once felt, long ago.

Patricia Leighton

Beaker Burial

Oh, it's no fun being under
a blooming great megalith
when you've got no one
to be
dead
with.

Death wasn't quite so lonely
when every Ancient Brit
was headed for the good old
communal
cremation
pit.

Then came the Beaker Folk
over the wave;
they said, 'From now on, son,
it's one man
one
grave.'

Curled up like a foetus,
I rot and complain;
just me and my beakers
under
Salisbury
Plain.

Vicki Raymond

*A megalith is a huge block of stone, used
in ancient monuments.*

*We don't know what the first people
to build round burial mounds called
themselves, so they have become known
as the 'Beaker People.' This is because
of the distinctive pottery 'beakers'
that they made and used.*

The Amphitheatre at Deva

They love the sight of the arena floor,
They love the crowd, screaming out for more,
They love two blades of Dimacherus
They love gold armoured Hoplomachius
They love to watch as others kill
They love to see condemned blood spill
They love to bet the beasts succeed
They love to see the horror freed
They love Samnite's speedy blows
They love Secutor's armoured clothes
They love the fact that slaves can die
They love to hear the pain filled cry
They love to see the Christian dead
They love the sight of a severed head
They love to watch Retarius fish
They love the net, and its deadly swish
They love to see the trident stab
They love to feel the excitement grab,
They love the clash of sword and spear
They love to feel the loser's fear

They love Mirmillo's massive shields
They love the curved sword Thracian wields
They love to see the new guy win
They love the hero's victory grin
They love the Velite's lightning strike
They love Laquearius' whip and pike
They love the stories that we tell
They love the theatre's morbid smell
They love the sand with bloody stains,
They love the death that entertains.

Jason Hulme

*'Deva' was the Roman name of Chester.
Dimacherus, Hoplomachius, Samnite, Secutor, Retarius,
Mirmillo, Thracian, Velite and Laquearius were various
types of gladiators, each with different skills.*

Roman Bath

Have a hot bath, a hot bath relaxes.
    Who cares if you can't afford to pay taxes?
    Who cares if your slaves start to riot and revolt?
    Who cares if you've run out of spices or salt?

Have a hot bath, a hot bath revives.
    Who cares if brown bears have eaten your hives
    and you can't sell your honey around the town?
    Who cares if the Emperor gives you 'thumbs down'?

Have a hot bath, a hot bath is best.
    Here's Pompeiian pumice and perfume – just rest.
    Who cares if barbarians disturb the 'pax'?
    Have a hot bath. Relax.

Mike Johnson

Roman Wall Blues

Over the heather the wet wind blows,
I've lice in my tunic and a cold in my nose.

The rain comes pattering out of the sky,
I'm a Wall soldier, I don't know why.

The mist creeps over the hard grey stone,
My girl's in Tungria; I sleep alone.

Aulus goes hanging around her place,
I don't like his manners, I don't like his face.

Piso's a Christian, he worships a fish;
There'd be no kissing if he had his wish.

She gave me a ring but I diced it away;
I want my girl and I want my pay.

When I'm a veteran with only one eye
I shall do nothing but look at the sky.

W.H. Auden

Hadrian's Wall ran for about 70 miles in length across Northern Britain from the North Sea to the Irish Sea. It was built to keep out the Picts and other warlike tribes who continually invaded from the north. For a Roman soldier, Hadrian's Wall was a bleak and lonely place.

A Pict Song

Rome never looks where she treads.
   Always her heavy hooves fall
On our stomachs, our hearts or our heads;
   And Rome never heeds when we bawl.
Her sentries pass on – that is all,
   And we gather behind them in hordes,
And plot to reconquer the Wall,
   With only our tongues for our swords.

We are the Little Folk – we!
   Too little to love or to hate.
Leave us alone and you'll see
   How we can drag down the State!
We are the worm in the wood!
   We are the rot at the root!
We are the taint in the blood!
   We are the thorn in the foot!

Mistletoe killing an oak –
   Rats gnawing cables in two –
Moths making holes in a cloak –
   How they must love what they do!
Yes – and we Little Folk too,
   We are busy as they –
Working our works out of view –
   Watch, and you'll see it some day!

No indeed! We are not strong,
  But we know Peoples that are.
Yes, and we'll guide them along
  To smash and destroy you in War!
We shall be slaves just the same?
  Yes, we have always been slaves,
But you – you will die of the shame,
  And then we shall dance on your graves!

We are the Little Folk – we!
  Too little to love or to hate.
Leave us alone and you'll see
  How we can drag down the State!
We are the worm in the wood!
  We are the rot at the root!
We are the taint in the blood!
  We are the thorn in the foot!

Rudyard Kipling

The Celts

They lived in France and Germany
   The Celts
They lived in France and Germany
   The Celts
They spread their community
Through Holland, Spain and Italy
They left their mark on history
   The Celts.

They moved around for centuries
   The Celts
They moved around for centuries
   The Celts
They moved on land, they moved on sea
From Africa to Brittany
They had great fun in Anglesey
   The Celts.

They worked with silver, bronze and gold
    The Celts
They worked with silver, bronze and gold
    The Celts
The goods they made were bought and sold
Then thrown away when they got old
And they made lucky charms to hold
    The Celts.

They were very agricultural
    The Celts
They were very agricultural
    The Celts
They were functional and pastoral
And really quite exceptional
And they were three-dimensional
    The Celts.

They had a great big empire
  The Celts
They had a great big empire
  The Celts
But just like every empire
For sure it had to expire
They even reigned in Hertfordshire
  The Celts.

They never had an emperor
  The Celts
They never had an emperor
  The Celts
They made homes in Macedonia
Turkey and Transylvania
But they never had an emperor
  The Celts.

They loved their oral poetry
  The Celts
They loved their oral poetry
  The Celts
A great night in for them you see
Was listening to a good story
They really used their memory
  The Celts.

They have languages that still survive
  The Celts
They have languages that still survive
  The Celts
They are a tough and sturdy tribe
In Wales and Scotland they survive
And in Ireland they really thrive
  The Celts.

Benjamin Zephaniah

Two Anglo-Saxon Riddles

I

On earth there's a warrior of curious origin.
He's created, gleaming, by two dumb creatures
for the benefit of men. Foe bears him against foe
to inflict harm. Women often fetter him,
strong as he is. If maidens and men
care for him with due consideration
and feed him frequently, he'll faithfully obey them
and serve them well. Men succour him for the warmth
he offers in return; but this warrior will savage
anyone who permits him to become too proud.

The Anglo-Saxons entertained each other with riddles after their feasts. The answers are at the bottom of the page.

Answer: fire

II

I'm by nature solitary, scarred by spear
and wounded by sword, weary of battle.
I frequently see the face of war, and fight
hateful enemies; yet I hold no hope
of help being brought to me in battle,
before I'm eventually done to death.
In the stronghold of the city sharp-edged swords,
skilfully forged in the flame by smiths,
bite deeply into me. I can but await
a more fearsome encounter; it is not for me
to discover in the city any of those doctors
who heal grievous wounds with roots and herbs.
The scars from sword wounds gape wider and wider;
death blows are dealt me by day and by night.

Kevin Crossley Holland

Answer: shield

Screamasax

Dragon-tongue
Bitter-biter
Blood-slaker
Hero-maker
Battle-brother
Death-dancer
Rune-carver
Iron-ogre
Screamasax

Diane Schneider

A screamasax was a Viking short sword.

*This poem is an example of a kenning where the writer
describes something in a number of vivid ways without actually
mentioning what is being described. It was a favourite technique
in Anglo-Saxon and Viking literature.*

A Viking Prays to his Gods

Great Niord, ruler of winds and seas,
The rain from heaven and the shining sun,
Guide our prows true over the waves,
Bring our ships safely to shore.

Mighty Thor, invincible warrior,
Thunderous hammer of the gods,
Help us to wield sword and axe with valour,
To die bravely if we must.

Lord Frey, crop guarder, race guarder,
Bless our winter fires with ease,
Protect our homelands, our people,
While we are sailing summer seas.

Freya, lady of plenty, receiver of heroes,
Bless our ventures with good luck.
And should we stay, settle, build new hearths,
Look kindly on us. Do not forget.

Great Odin, father of all, never desert us.
Wherever our sons ship oars,
Whether they plough sea or earth,
May there always be salt in their blood

Valhalla on their horizons.

Patricia Leighton

*Valhalla was the hall of the gods, where Odin lived with all
the warriors who had been slain in battle.*

Bitter Winds

T
O
N
I
G
H
T

the wind is an angry bear –
it tosses and tumbles
Old Sea's white hair.
Tonight, we shield from
the piercing spears of rain

A
N
D

the sword sharp wind – our North Sea bane.
Yet, tonight, it is the stormy sea which saves,
for no fierce Norse warriors
will wade ashore through
those wild
waves.

Tim Pointon

This shape poem is based on a Dark Ages poem written by an Irish monk in the margin of his book, which reads:

> *Bitter is the wind tonight,*
> *It tosses the ocean's white hair:*
> *Tonight I fear not the fierce warriors of Norway*
> *Coursing on the Irish Sea.*

Question asked in the Yorvik Centre:

When did the Vikings leave York?
Answer: We never did.

Through the glitter of the grey
North Sea, we cut a shining furrow
Parting the waves with a dragon prow.
And now we're here
Rooted in the earth we plough.

The sea that rose in green salt hills
Silver with herring harvest
Still fills my dreams
But daylight brings me to a farm
A field of spelt, a pig
A neat black cow.
I'm settled now.

And spread into this place
Our names are your names
Your hair shines red like ours
We share a family face.

Jan Dean

At Senlac Hill,
15th October, 1066

Broken blades still bright with blood
fallen and flung far over the field,
the battered bodies of mangled men,
beaten by battle, bruised and bleeding
crying for care, or still as stones
their shields shattered, their spears scattered,
their breathing butchered, spent and stopped,
lie heaped and piled in many mounds.

My sister and I search for our father
killed or captured, we don't know
but missing since midnight,
like Harold our King, now carrion crows
swoop and swirl over the fallen
pecking for pickings, our mother moans,
weeps in her hands and holds her hair
away from her face, missing her man
amongst the many, the stiff and the still
or those who groan from their war-wounds.

Yesterday we were Saxons, English and angry
ready for riot against our foes
now we are Norman, French and fatherless
dazed and despairing, lost with the dead
already our masters make preparations
digging their ditches to raise their ramparts
our future is dreaded, dismal and dull
stretched out in front of us like a dark day.

David Harmer

*The Battle of Hastings was fought at Senlac Hill on
14 October, 1066. King Harold and his army were
defeated by the French invaders led by William the
Conqueror. Senlac Hill, by the way, is not part of
present-day Hastings, it is six miles away in the
town of Battle!*

Encourage the Oxen

A ploughman has no cause for gloom,
he should sing and be cheerful,
encourage the oxen with his song.

He needs to take feed and straw
for his cattle, to make a fuss of them
and always treat them well.

He needs to brush them and curry them,
be fond of these beasts –
stay in the stable with them at night.

Joan Poulson

*This poem is based on a thirteenth-century recommendation
to ploughmen by 'Walter of Henley'.*

King John

John was a tyrant,
John was a tartar,
But John put his name to the Great Big Charter.
Every Baron,
From Thames to Tweed,
Followed the road
To Runnymede.
Every Baron had something to say
To poor perplexed King John that day.
'Pray sign your name,' said Guy de Gaunt;
'It's easily done, and it's all we want.'
'A *J* and an *O* and an *H* and an *N*,'
Said Hugo, Baron of Harpenden.
Quietly spoke the Lord Rambure:
'Oblige, Lord King, with your signature.'
'Your name, my liege, to be writ just here,
A mere formality,' laughed de Bere.
'A stroke of the pen and the thing is done,'
Murmured Sir Roger of Trumpington.
'Done in a twinkling,' sniffed de Guise.
Said Stephen Langton: 'Sign, if you please!'
So many people
Egged him on,
I can't help feeling
Sorry for John.

Hugh Chesterman

Battle of Falkirk, 1298

To: Edward, King of England

Sire,
I am your humble subject, and an old soldier
that fought with you in battles past.
News has come to me from Falkirk.
The 'Hammer of the Scots' has struck again
and I rejoice in your victory.

And yet my heart is troubled.
I fear the manner of that victory
may leave a stain upon your memory.
I refer to your use of the long-bow.

I faced the enemy with sword and shield.
In the cut and thrust of battle
I gave wounds and received them.
I knew the fear and fierce joy of conflict
and prayed for the souls of those whose blood I spilt.

Your archers never saw their foe.
They shot showers of arrows in the air
that fell on men like deadly rain, indiscriminate.
Weapons of mass destruction.
Thousands died with none to know
who loosed the fatal shaft.

Let us fight, if fight we must, manfully
and look our enemy in the eye.
Let he who cannot do it stay at home
not cower behind a bended piece of yew.
I beg of you, my lord, to cease this practice.
Let courage be the order of the day.
If war means nothing more than pulling strings
where will it end?

I am your majesty's true liege-man,

Thomas Greenwood

[Written at the behest of the above by Geoffrey
  Coombes, Clerk.]

Gus Grenfell

*The Battle of Falkirk was one of a series of battles in the Scottish
wars of independence. The Scots, under William Wallace
(Braveheart) were expecting to fight the huge English force at
close quarters. They were quite unprepared for King Edward's
new tactic of firing arrows from the distance into the tight
formations of Scottish spearmen.*

*Edward I called himself 'The Hammer of the Scots'. He had it
engraved in Latin on his tomb in Westminster Abbey. He was
generally known as 'Longshanks', because he was six feet two
inches (nearly two metres) tall.*

King Robert The Bruce: The Spider Replies

'For a King he was really depressing,
he mumbled and muttered and moaned.
He was miserable, mournful and mopey
and if spiders could groan, I'd have groaned.

I said, "Look, Jock," but he didn't answer –
he didn't speak "Spider", you see,
but one thing did catch his attention,
my woven web's intricacy.

He studied my efforts for hours.
I was having a terrible day
on account of him staring right at me,
"Get lost, King," I said, "Go away."

He so put me off but he didn't budge,
for where do Kings go when they're down?
I had my patterns and pictures to plan,
he'd lost his meaning … and crown.

Yet somehow I think I inspired him,
he went on to greatness and gold.
I stayed behind unrewarded
in the dark, and the damp, and the cold.

And many remember his courage,
he's a high point on history's graph.
As for me I was just a mere spider,
like the one you might find in your bath.
For we're not regarded as regal
with castles and paintings to spare.
We're meagre and measly and minor . . .

. . . who hang works of art in mid-air. '

Stewart Henderson

*Legend tells us that a former king of Scotland, Robert The Bruce,
after being defeated in battle, ran for his life and hid in a cave.
There he watched a spider make six attempts to climb a web.
On the seventh attempt the spider succeeded, which encouraged
Robert The Bruce to go out and regain his crown.*

Tod Boucher, 1378

Here's Tod Boucher in the pillory:
mucky owd clod!

Laugh at him, laugh at him,
chuck a bit o' fat at him!

Fined for selling measled meat,
he was, and well deserves his fate:

them stinking lumps humped
round his neck and tight-secured.

They say as dogs had ripped
and gnawed at it afore he got it.

Greedy owd Boucher, taking
our hard-earned farthings
for little more than dog leavings.

Joan Poulson

Tod Boucher is a name taken from
a fourteenth-century manuscript.

FROM THE CANTERBURY TALES

A Knight

A Knight there was, and that a worthy man,
Who, from the moment when he first began
To ride forth, loved the code of chivalry:
Honour and truth, freedom and courtesy.
His lord's war had established him in worth;
He rode – and no man further – ends of earth
In heathen parts as well as Christendom,
Honoured wherever he might go or come...
Of mortal battles he had seen fifteen,
And fought hard for our faith at Tramassene
Thrice in the lists, and always slain his foe.
This noble knight was even led to go
To Turkey where he fought most valiantly
Against the heathen hordes for Palaty.
Renowned he was; and, worthy, he was wise –
Prudence, with him, was more than mere disguise;
He was as meek in manner as a maid.
Vileness he shunned, rudeness he never said
In all his life, respecting each man's right.
He was a truly perfect, noble knight.

A Squire

With him there was his son, a youthful Squire,
A merry blade, a love full of fire;
With locks as curled as though laid in a press –
Scarce twenty years of age was he, I guess.
In stature he was of an average length,
Wondrously active, bright, and great in strength.
He proved himself a soldier handsomely
In Flanders, in Artois and Picardy,
Bearing himself so well, in so short space,
Hoping to stand high in his lady's grace.
Embroidered was his clothing, like a bed
Full of gay flowers, shining white and red.
Singing he was, or fluting, all the day –
He was as fresh as is the month of May.
Short was his gown; his sleeves were long and wide;
Well did he sit his horse, and nimbly ride,
He could make songs, intone them or indite,
Joust, play and dance, and also draw and write.
So well could he repeat love's endless tale,
He slept no more than does the nightingale.
Yet he was humble, courteous and able,
And carved before his father when at table.

A Miller

The Miller, stout and sturdy as the stones,
Delighted in his muscles and big bones;
They served him well; at fair and tournament
He took the wrestling prize where'er he went.
He was short-shouldered, broad, knotty and tough;
He'd tear a door down easily enough
Or break it, charging thickly with his head.
His beard, like any sow or fox, was red,
And broadly built, as though it were a spade.
Upon the tiptop of his nose he had
A wart, and thereon stood a tuft of hairs,
Bright as the bristles of a red sow's ears.
His nostrils matched the miller, black and wide.
He bore a sword and buckler by his side.
His mouth was broad as a great furnace door.
He loved to tell a joke, and boast, and roar
About his many sins and deviltries;
He stole, and multiplied his thefts by threes.
And yet he had a thumb of gold, 'tis true.
He wore a white coat and a hood of blue,
And he could blow the bagpipe up and down –
And with a tune he brought us out of town.

Geoffrey Chaucer
[Modern Version by Louis Untermeyer]

The Canterbury Tales *were composed by Geoffrey Chaucer*
around 1386–1400. The tales describe some of the pilgrims who
travel on the annual April pilgrimage to Canterbury Cathedral.
They give us an interesting picture of fourteenth-century England.

Cry God for Harry

Daddy, what did you do at Agincourt?
Slogged through fields of mud.

Dad, did you kill many Frenchmen?
Waded through their blood.

Was it exciting, was it fun?
No, it was pretty gruesome, son!

Dog-tired, hungry, dragging along
Troubled souls and shields,
Outnumbered, laughed at by the French,
We longed for English fields
And hedgerows sweet with hawthorn
Where blackbirds, thrushes dart
And larks go spiralling upwards
With songs that thrill the heart.

But, Daddy, it was glorious:
When you sailed back over the sea
The bells of England all announced
A Famous Victory.

Well, son, I will say this:
If Henry hadn't spurred us on,
Pumped up our adrenalin,
We Englishmen would not have won...
It was against all possible odds.
Let's say the victory was God's!
But, then, all armies always claim
Slaughter's done in God's good name.

Matt Simpson

The Battle of Agincourt was fought against the French
in 1415. King Henry V and his army were victorious.

Silence at Meals
(a 15th-century Monastery)

At meal-times we sit in the Hall
with the Prior and the Monks,
and we're not allowed to speak a word.
Imagine getting people to pass things
using sign-language and gesticulating
and mouthing like actors overdoing it,
even doing mime-writing on the table,
just to say: *Which kind of fish,*
Brother Michael, roast or stuffed?
It's quite a sight, all the pointing
and making shapes and nodding
and head-shaking and face-pulling.
More Venison, Brother James?
It looks like a mad-house at first
but you soon get used to it –
and start to understand things.
Today I had to tell Brother Thomas:
Leave some roast thrushes
for me, Thomas, please.

Then Bernard and Thomas started
sending messages to each other:
Please will you pass the basil
and not be so difficult? Why is this
smothered in eggs and pepper?
Wine with your water? Yesterday
at dinner Brother Mark pretended
to send a danger signal down the table:
Avoid the cockles, brothers!
Brother Septimus was funniest though.
This wine's so full of dregs
I've had to keep my teeth closed.
Then he did a panic expression at Jonathan.
Brother Jonathan, your cod's four days old!
I saw it on Tuesday in the market!
I'd recognise that face anywhere!
I nearly burst out laughing in front of the Prior.

Robert Hull

Bosworth Field

And I saw the dead and wounded
Crying here and beyond the grave,
And I asked me, 'Was it worth it?
Was this all worthwhile to save
The crown, the preserved lineage?
To make this country free,
Or were they martyred for the gain
Of no one else but me?'

My nobles gathered, 'Victory, Sire,
More glory on this day!'
But emptiness within my heart,
I bade them go away
And ponder on the present,
'Thus it was!' I said,
'Would now you say such glory
If you were those,
Those dead?'

Ian Larmont

*The Battle of Bosworth Field took place in Leicestershire,
in 1485. The battle ended over 30 years of civil war, when
King Richard III was defeated by Henry Tudor, who became
the first Tudor king (Henry VII).*

Anne Boleyn
A Legend of the Tower of London

Her little feet in scarlet shoon
They made a pleasant sound
Across the pavement where the moon
Drew patterns on the ground.

Her clenchèd fists so small and white
Went beating on the door,
The oaken door that to her sight
Would open, never more.

She knelt upon the grey cold stone,
And bowed her head in tears;
She wept, because her heart had grown
Too wild to hide its fears.

'O Harry love, O dear my King
I prithee let me in;
Thou couldst not do this cruel thing
To merry Anne Boleyn.'

She fluttered like some wounded lark
And ever called his name;
They chained her wrists and through the dark
They led her to her shame.

So young was she to die alone,
So fair, and full of tears,
So warm to rest beneath a stone
Through countless weary years,

That sometimes now men hear her feet
Across the tower floor,
Her voice beseech, her small hands beat
Upon that silent door.

'O Harry love, O dear my King
I prithee let me in;
Thou couldst not do this cruel thing
To merry Anne Boleyn.'

Barbara Bingley

Henry VIII married Anne Boleyn after he had divorced his first wife, Catherine of Aragon. Anne failed to produce a son and heir, and the king eventually had her executed.

Cardinal Wolsey

'How can I please you?'
The Cardinal smiled,
With his face so round
And his voice so mild.

> 'A King needs freedom,
> A King needs hope.
> You must grovel and pray
> At the feet of the Pope.'

'How can I please you?'
The Cardinal sighed,
With his crimson robes
And his injured pride.

> 'A King needs someone
> Who gets things done.
> I need a divorce
> Since I must have a son.'

'How can I please you?'
The Cardinal wailed,
With his message torn
And his mission failed.

'A King needs fanfares,
He needs success.
But all you have brought me
Is emptiness.'

'How can I please you?'
The Cardinal sobbed,
With his future wrecked
And his fortune robbed.

'A King needs a palace
With walls blood red,
And a Cardinal's land,
And a Cardinal's head.'

'I just couldn't please him,'
The Cardinal said
With his parched white lips.

And his heart stopped dead.

Clare Bevan

Last Wife
(Katherine Parr)

My hair is dressed by maids who chatter on;
I look into my mirror, breathe a sigh.
My wedding day has come, all choice has gone;
The King demands my hand, I must comply.

Two husbands have I known and there's no doubt
As Henry's wife I'll need to tend him well.
He battles daily 'gainst the dreadful pain of gout
With body huge, his legs soon puff and swell.

A nursemaid more I'll be, as well as Queen:
A mother to his children who need care.
I want to give support yet what of me?
Too young – my fate now leads I know not where.

And what if I should next displease the King?
The Tower may become my home e'er long
Or worse, what change of fortune will I bring
Upon my head, if I should somehow fail and do him wrong?

My mirror shakes within my jewelled hand
The trumpets sound, 'tis time to make my way.
I rise in hope that I'll help Henry stand
And live to see him smile on me each day.

Lyn Gregory

Katherine Parr was the last of Henry VIII's six wives. She nursed the king in his final years and outlived him.

Lady Jane Grey

Lady Jane Grey
   Went on her way
Out of her house
   On the first of May.

The blackbird whistled,
   The blackbird sang
And all the bells
   Of England rang.

She went to the palace.
   She sat her down.
She wore the Queen
   Of England's crown.

She wore it a week
   And a day and a day
Of her sixteen years,
   Poor Lady Jane Grey.

Charles Causley

Edward VI was only 16 years old when he died in 1553. Henry VIII's Catholic daughter, Mary, was the rightful queen and to stop her gaining the throne, a group of powerful nobles tried to make Lady Jane Grey the next Queen of England. The plotters were defeated and Mary had Lady Jane executed.

Love Letter from Mary Tudor

to her Husband, Philip of Spain

Dear Philip, my Phil
  it's making me ill
to think that
  you don't love me.
I love you, my dear
  but you're making it clear
that this marriage
  was not meant to be.

I'm here all alone,
  if only you'd call,
send a pigeon
  or simply just write.
Invite me, please do,
  Ibiza with you
would soon set
  our marriage alight.

Dear Philip, my love,
  my sweet turtle dove,
I know it's with you
  I relate.
I wish you'd return
  and help me to burn
all those plotting
  against the state.

Everybody I know
    says you should go,
but I need you
    to give me an heir.
Do you think that I'm neater
    than a sweet senorita
or do your eyes
    wander elsewhere?

Dear Philip, I'm willing
    to share double-billing,
if our love could be
    reignited.
Then our reign as one
    will be equal to none,
King and Queen of
    two countries united.

So Philip, my Phil,
    come home, say you will,
without you it's really
    quite scary.
Forsake sunny Spain
    for the cold English rain
and the arms of
    your loving wife, Mary.

XXXX

Brian Moses

*Mary married the Catholic Philip of Spain in
an attempt to unite Spain and England. However,
her husband decided that he was not very keen on his
new wife and chose to spend most of his time in Spain.*

Stowaway!

When we set sail I was hiding;
Squashed between oak barrels in the hold
As the ship left Plymouth for the second time.
I knew many had come to cheer us away,
Waving and calling:
'God Speed the *Pelican*,' and 'God Bless Drake'.
My heart leapt with pride; my stomach also leapt full well
As we lurched and rolled into deeper waters.

Soon a sailor heard me retching,
Dragged me before the General and I, green faced,
Held myself upright with difficulty before him.
'Shall we flog him?' Drake asked the assembled men,
'Or tie him to the mainstay for the birds to feast upon...?'
I felt my legs flounder – then, glancing up, did note
Such a sea of laughing faces,
As the crew joined in his joking.

'He'll work like the rest, Sir,' a sober voice replied:
My Uncle, Francis Pretty,
Fixed me with an unpretty stare
And tugged his golden ear-hoop angrily.
'I'll see he earns his keep!' –
And as sure as Elizabeth is Queen, he did.

I learned fast the ways of the sea, the knots and rigging;
Got to taste the cocos at Magellen, eat the flesh of sea wolves
And wonder at the herb called Tabah
The natives gave us in exchange for cloth.
I was on deck when we lost the *Marigold* in a storm
And still smooth for want of a beard
When we were the only ship left of the five;
A *Golden Hind* with no companion stags.

But never did the General waiver – we *would* sail the world
And Her Majesty would savour the golden bounty
Of Spanish coins we took from *Cacafuego's* hold...
(Such rum we drank that night!)
I was now accustomed to its fiery burn
As Spain became to our burning of her ships.

Us, pirates?
Never! We just pleased Her Majesty full well,
Supplying her with delights and trinkets rare.
Rather call us 'Protectors of the Realm,'
And remember there was none so devoted in his turn
As me, young John, stowaway on the *Golden Hind!*

Lyn Gregory

The Pelican *was re-named the* Golden Hind *at the Straits of
Magellen, the hind being the crest of Sir Christopher Hatton.
(Francis Pretty, one of Drake's gentlemen-at-arms on board,
wrote detailed accounts of this voyage. The* Marigold *was one of
five vessels to set sail round the world in 1577. All were lost in
storms, except the* Elizabeth, *which went home and the* Golden
Hind, *which went on alone.*

The Cacafuego, *a Spanish ship, was chased and ransacked by
Drake in the South Pacific on this voyage, providing a huge
bounty of gold and jewels. Elizabeth I turned a blind eye to the
pirating exploits of her favoured explorers, her Protectors of the
Realm, choosing to accept the bounty with no questions asked.*

Cocos – coconuts
Sea wolves – seals
Tabah – tobacco

Fireships

Pack away, pack away
all that will burn:
rags, oil and timber
from bow through to stern.

Sneak away, sneak away
sneak through the night
with volunteer crews
to set them alight.

Row away, row away,
ships now on fire,
a threat to the Spanish,
a danger most dire.

Cut away, cut away,
cut anchors free:
see Spaniards struggle
to flee out to sea.

Sail away, sail away,
escape English fleet;
the day will soon dawn
on Armada's defeat.

Rowena M. Love

*Fireships played a big part in defeating the Spanish Armada in
1558. These ships were deliberately set on fire and then set on
course for the Spanish fleet.*

To See –
Or Not To See

(An Interview with Richard Burbage, Actor)

We've constructed 'The Globe'
Out of wood and from thatch
In the shape of an 'O'
On a really *fine* patch
With a wide OPEN roof –
Yes, alas! – *that's* the catch,
For a theatre needs plenty of light.

And people know when
A performance is due,
For a flag is displayed
If the sky's clear and blue;
We've courtiers, beggars
And pickpockets, too,
Who flock to each 'opening night'.

The plays we perform
Are from Will Shakespeare's pen
And my actors are called
'The Lord Chamberlain's Men'
And our public seems happy
Ten times out of ten,
With plays both in prose *and* in rhyme.

The charge is one penny
For 'groundlings' (those who
Stand in the open
And shout, cheer or boo!);
But a gallery seat
For the more 'well-to-do'
Will set you back three pence a time.

Overhead, on the stage,
Are 'The Heavens' (in paint) –
While, beneath us, lurks 'Hell'
And a few patrons faint
If 'Devils' appear
Through the traps, which is 'quaint'
(Though I think a trifle *insane!*)

And out of 'The Heavens'
A throne may descend,
Cranked upon chains,
Its 'creaks' timed to blend
With sounds from the Turret
The stage-hands intend
Should indicate 'thunder' or 'rain'!

Oh, no –
Here comes a REAL cloudburst again!

(With no roof for cover,
If the sky starts to dim,
For most of our patrons
The 'outlook' is *grim*...!)

Sorry, 'groundlings' –
It looks like you're in for *another* soaking!

Trevor Harvey

Burbage's father, James, built the first public theatre ('The Theatre') at Shoreditch, on the outskirts of the City of London in 1577. In 1599, it was dismantled and most of its timbers were used to construct a new theatre, 'The Globe', on the South Bank of the Thames, with Richard's brother, Cuthbert, as manager. They staged new plays by William Shakespeare and other playwrights.

61

Bess's Bath

With pails of hot water the ladies in waiting
run up the stairs.
The courtiers sniff at their scented pomanders,
the ambassadors laugh
they think it so weird: for the third time this year
Elizabeth Tudor is taking a bath.

In the royal bedchamber the queen sits in state
in her steamy tub,
she's removed her red wig to rub her head better
with ring-crusted fingers
and scrubbed the white powder from her face to reveal
care-worn wrinkles and smallpox scars.

Through teeth blackened by sugar she starts to whistle
and says in her heart:
'I may not have Mary Stewart's looks (or her neck),
but she never sees soap,
and Philip of Spain may be filthy rich, but today
I'm the cleanest monarch in Europe.'

Dave Calder

James I
1603

James the First is now the king
I'll help you in remembering.

Please remember James was not
An English monarch, but a Scot.

Also, James had goggle eyes,
And drank more liquor than was wise.

James the First it was who sold
Titles in return for gold.

Furthermore, he took a pride
In hunting, though he couldn't ride.

But if James the First you'd fix
So that in your mind he sticks,

Then remember, in his reign,
Guy Fawkes tried, and tried in vain,

With gunpowder to explode
The Parliamentary abode.

So, my child, when you and I,
Lighting fireworks, think of Guy,

Let us, 'mid the pretty flames,
Remember to remember James.

Eleanor and Herbert Farjeon

'They Shall Receive a Great Blow'

I was the boy on the lumbering cart
creaking over the darkened cobbles
that night with my father and the man
I later knew as Mr Fawkes.

'I'm Johnson,' he said 'You come with me.'
The cart was so heavy, the horse so tired
worn out by the journey, pulling the load
of barrels and brushwood, coals and kindling.

I asked my father if it was right
to load all this stuff into the cellars
right there, under the House of Lords.
I wondered, all this gunpowder and fuel –
wasn't it dangerous? It could all go bang.

You see, I didn't understand
and all I got was a thump round the ear.
'Be quiet,' they said, the men in the cloaks
hats pulled low, voices a mutter,
'It isn't explosives, just sand and dust.'
But I knew different, saw it spill
on to the floor from a loosening bung
when we trundled in the last barrel.

It wasn't my father and it wasn't me
who betrayed the plotters to the guard.
It came from a letter, that was how
they caught Guy Fawkes with his hand on the match,
the slow sizzling snake of sparks
starting to crawl towards the explosion.

They took him and hanged him
pulled out his guts
everything happened in front of my eyes.
Yes, I was the boy who saw it all
the boy who said nothing
who kept his mouth shut.

David Harmer

The Children
of Witches

Mark is the son of a blacksmith,
John's folk keep pigs and dig ditches,
but Robert and Jessie and me,
we are the children of witches.

Mark is an expert at hunting,
John wins at games of chance,
but Robert and Jessie and me,
we saw the witches dance.

Mark is as tough as an anvil,
John has wings on his feet,
but Robert and Jessie and me,
we know where the witches meet.

Mark sings aloud in the choir,
John prays at home every day,
but Robert and Jessie and me,
we gave the witches away.

We were easily tricked by questions,
was it truth we should tell or a lie?
So we told tales on the witches
and condemned our mothers to die.

Soon Mark will start work in the smithy
while John helps his father dig ditches.
But there's no certain future for any of those
who are tainted as children of witches.

Brian Moses

*During the witchcraft trials of the early seventeenth
century, the evidence of children was considered
acceptable. Judges were keen to make as may
convictions as they could in order to please King
James I, who considered himself an expert on
the matter.*

Landing of the Pilgrim Fathers

The breaking waves dashed high,
  On a stern and rock-bound coast,
And the woods against a stormy sky,
  Their giant branches tossed;

And the heavy night hung dark,
  The hills and waters o'er,
When a band of exiles moored their bark
  On the wild New England shore.

Not as the conqueror comes,
  They, the true-hearted came;
Not with the roll of the stirring drums,
  And the trumpet that sings of fame;

Not as the flying come,
  In silence and in fear –
They shook the depths of the desert gloom
  With their hymns of lofty cheer.

Amidst the storm they sang,
  And the stars heard, and the sea;
And the sounding aisles of the dim woods rang
  To the anthem of the free.

The ocean eagle soared
　　From his nest by the white wave's foam;
And the rocking pines of the forest roared –
　　This was their welcome home.

There were men with hoary hair
　　Amidst that pilgrim band:
Why had they come to wither there,
　　Away from their childhood's land?

There was a woman's fearless eye,
　　Lit by her deep love's truth;
There was a manhood's brow serenely high,
　　And the firey heart of youth.

What sought they thus afar?
　　Bright jewels of the mine?
The wealth of seas, the spoils of war?
　　They sought a faith's pure shrine!

Aye, call it holy ground,
　　The soil where first they trod;
They have left unstained what there they found –
　　Freedom to worship God.

Felicia Hemans

The Pilgrim Fathers were a group of men and women known as Puritans, who left England in 1620 to find a place where they could worship freely. They reached the American continent and founded a new settlement there.

The Priest Hole

Forget about the priest hole, sister.
Do not let your feet
Tap the hollow floorboards
Beside the chimney seat.

Forget about the priest hole, sister.
Do not let your face
Seek the rusty hinges
That mark his hiding place.

Forget about the priest hole, sister.
Do not let your eyes
Slide towards the shadows
Or signal where he lies.

Forget about the priest hole, sister.
Do not let your mind
Tiptoe down the tunnel
The soldiers came to find.

Forget about the priest hole, sister.
Do not let your fear
Shine as pale as moonlight
To draw the hunters near.

Forget about the priest hole, sister.
Do not let your heart
Thunder like a war drum –
Until the men depart.

Clare Bevan

Many houses were built with hiding places where someone could hide in times of religious persecution. These 'priest holes' as they became known, were put to good use in the English Civil War.

Homecoming 1648

How can I bear to let him touch me now
feel his hand on my skin
knowing what he has done?
Yet I am his wife and
have borne his sons, but
how can I bear to let him touch me now?

When after three days' fighting
he returned from Preston
his eyes could not meet mine.
He spoke of his near death
told how outnumbered Royalists
fought to the last man.

Hours dragged by before he spoke again
but I forebore to question
fearing what might come;
since this war began
brother has fought brother
and friendships have been broken on the battlefield.

History has often witnessed evil
but history knows no father
and history has no heart.
Now when my husband takes a knife
to carve a piece of beef
I vision my father's throat stabbed by that same hand.

Peggy Poole

*The Battle of Preston, in August 1648, was the last big battle of
the Civil War. The war had gone on for six years, often bitterly
dividing families all over Britain.*

Night Thoughts of Oliver Cromwell

I signed the death warrant that finished the King,
My name was third on the list.

He ruled without parliament, for power and gain,
He taxed and demanded and never explained,
He schemed with the Catholics and Ireland and Spain
And stirred up unrest in the country.
We Parliamentarians had to take charge,
Under God, our duty was clear,
To bring in a new constitution by law,
That would stand through the tests of the years,
And guarantee peace for the country.

We were right, I am sure, and I have no regrets,
The future is now with the people,

But sometimes, it seems in the still of the night
That time stops in the heart of my being,
And all that exists is this sentence of mine,
That I signed for the death of the King.

Daphne Kitching

Oliver Cromwell
1653

Down with actors! Down with plays!
Such the cry in Cromwell's days!
Down with puppets! Down with sport!
Down with fun of every sort!
Tightrope-walking, football, cricket,
Even bowls is counted wicked!
England's governed by objectors!
Lord protect us from Protectors!

Now are jesters all suppressed!
Cap and bells must take a rest!
No more wrestling on the green
Or grinning matches now are seen!
Now the merry maypole's hidden!
Christmas puddings are forbidden!
Oh, these circumspect inspectors!
Lord protect us from Protectors!

Eleanor and Herbert Farjeon

The Cries of London

Here's fine rosemary, sage and thyme.
Come buy my ground ivy.
Here's fetherfew, gilliflowers and rue.
Come buy my knotted marjorum, ho!
Come buy my mint, my fine green mint.
Here's fine lavender for your cloaths.
Here's parsley and winter-savory,
And hearts-ease, which all do choose.
Here's balm and hissop, and cinquefoil,
All fine herbs, it is well known.
    Let none despise the merry, merry cries
    Of famous London-town!

Here's fine herrings, eight a groat.
Hot codlins, pies and tarts.
New mackerel! have to sell.
Come buy my Wellfleet oysters, ho!
Come buy my whitings fine and new.
Wives, shall I mend your husbands horns?
I'll grind your knives to please your wives,
And very nicely cut your corns.
Maids, have you any hair to sell,
Either flaxen, black, or brown?
    Let none despise the merry, merry cries
    Of famous London-town!

Anonymous

Place of the Plague Wife

Today I stood inside the dry stone ring
which was your land. Despite three hundred years
that separate us, I can hear you sing
your epitaph and taste your salty tears.

Strengthened by constant toil, you must have plied
your husband's spade and cursed that foul disease
till aches and pains replaced the hurt inside.
Alone you watched and nursed, alone you knew
the hope you cherished shrivel as they died.

Did you pray for their souls, or that you too
could die as they did? Or did you stand back
to cry your loss and let your sobs ring through
the rock clefts, paint the landscape all in black?
Did call of cattle force your grieving heart
to concentrate on ordinary tasks?

Did you have strength enough to make you start
afresh when seven times your love lay deep
in earth? Or did pain drag your wits apart?

Colder than stones that mark their graves, you sleep
with them once more. Today a man could pass
this place, not sense the secret woe it keeps.

Today I knotted seven blades of grass –
a ring of roses to protect your rest.

Alison Chisholm

*This poem is for Mrs Hancocke, who buried a husband
and six children when the Plague attacked the Derbyshire
village of Eyam.*

The Fire of London, 1666

There had been city fires before
But this fire leapt like a dragon's roar
From a baker's shop in Pudding Lane,
Raged like a tiger, sending flames
Swift as thought from street to street,
Devouring houses with its heat,
Swallowing buildings, scattering sparks
Over the rooftops, churches, parks.
Crazed with success, the fire burned bright
For four long nightmare days and nights.
Boats crammed the waters of the Thames
As people tried to flee the flames,
While others watched in dread and fear,
As smoke and towering flames appeared
To block their path at every turn,
Threatening to consume and burn.
When, finally, the fire died down
Little remained of London town,
Its wooden buildings, narrow lanes,
Demolished by the ravenous flames.
But rising from the drifting ashes
Came spacious streets and palaces,
Stately buildings, marble halls,
And Wren's great masterpiece, St Paul's.

Cynthia Rider

Epitaph on Charles II

Here lies our Sovereign Lord the King,
    Whose word no man relies on,
Who never said a foolish thing,
    Nor ever did a wise one.

John Wilmot, Earl of Rochester

The Press-Gang

Here's the tender coming,
    Pressing all the men;
        O, dear honey,
    What shall we do then?
Here's the tender coming,
    Off at Shields Bar.
Here's the tender coming,
    Full of men of war.

Here's the tender coming,
    Stealing of my dear;
        O, dear honey,
They'll ship you out of here,
    They'll ship you foreign,
For that is what it means.
    Here's the tender coming,
Full of red marines.

Anonymous

The Press-Gang was a gang of sailors under an officer, empowered to impress men into the navy.

A tender was a small craft that attends a larger one.

Sea Dreaming, Grape Lane

How many nights adrift
in that ship-timbered attic
did he dream salt? The creak
of ropes that held his hammock
echoed rigging noises; as he swung
each chill shift of air breathed
promises of tropic breezes.

How often did he wake
when the skylight flooded stars
became his porthole? – then lie
imagining their angles change
in skies above a rolling ship?

Did he hear mew of Whitby gulls
translated into monkey's cry,
parrot's squawk? Landlocked in winter,
did he pace the quay, his deck,
and gaze beyond the point
where slate sea and pewter sky met?

And when books – sole companions
of a solitary lad – yielded thoughts
to dance in candle's flicker,
were their pages charts of empty space
he had to fill? They teased his sleep,
tormented till the throb of sea
that pulsed his veins insisted:
Endeavour – Resolution – Adventure – Discovery.

Alison Chisholm

*As an apprentice, Captain James Cook lodged in Grape Lane,
Whitby. The last four words in this poem are the names of
Captain Cook's ships.*

My Extraordinary Life

Born an African,
I was kidnapped at the age of ten,
Sent to Virginia and sold to a planter.
From there I was purchased by the high seas
And the English Navy.

I served many masters for many years
Until I became my own master.

My name was Olaudah,
The voice,
Then I became Gustavus Vassa,
Or sometimes Michael
Or Jacob.

Those with many names are loved by the gods.

My journeys were remarkable.
I travelled to Belle-Isle, Cadiz, Gibraltar, Martinico,
Rode the Bahama Banks,
Sailed to Jamaica and the Musquito shore,
Slept under desert and ice moons,
Went north to the Pole and the land of the white bears,
The chill winds and the vast unbroken wastes.

As a free man
I took work in Central America
I bought men for the plantations.
A grim business, that,
Buying and selling myself.

And so I returned to England.

I travelled through Scotland and Ireland,
Wrote letters and essays in London,
Became a campaigner.
I railed against the neck-yoke, muzzle and chain,
The human cargo, pestilence and greed,
And set down...

The Interesting Narrative
Of
Olaudah Equiano
Or
Gustavus Vassa
The African
Written by Himself
1789

My extraordinary life.

I married Susanna, an English woman,
Had two daughters,
Anna Maria the eldest,
Joanna the youngest.
My deathbed was recorded.
My legacy inherited.

England had embraced me,
Given me kindness and brutality,
Had called me a gentleman,
But not an equal.

    Mary Green

> *Olaudah Equiano (1745–1797) was the African slave of an*
> *English naval officer for much of his early life. After great*
> *difficulty he managed to buy his freedom in 1766. His many*
> *experiences and views are recounted in his autobiography.*

A Smugglers' Song

If you wake at midnight and hear a horse's feet,
Don't go drawing back the blind, or looking down the street,
Them that asks no questions isn't told a lie.
Watch the wall, my darling, while the Gentlemen go by!
     Five and twenty ponies,
     Trotting through the dark –
     Brandy for the Parson,
     'Baccy for the Clerk;
     Laces for the lady; letters for a spy,
And watch the wall, my darling, while the Gentlemen go by!

Running round the woodlump if you chance to find
Little barrels, roped and tarred, all full of brandy-wine;
Don't you shout to come and look, nor take 'em for your
    play;
Put the brushwood back again – and they'll be gone next day!

If you see the stableyard setting open wide;
If you see a tired horse lying down inside;
If your mother mends a coat cut about and tore;
If the lining's wet and warm – don't you ask no more!

If you meet King George's men, dressed in blue and red,
You be careful what you say, and mindful what is said.
If they call you 'pretty maid', and chuck you 'neath the chin,
Don't you tell where no one is, nor yet where no one's been!

Knocks and footsteps round the house – whistles after dark –
You've no call for running out till the housedogs bark.
Trusty's here and Pincher's here, and see how dumb they lie –
They don't fret to follow when the Gentlemen go by!

If you do as you've been told, likely there's a chance,
You'll be give a dainty doll, all the way from France,
With a cap of Valenciennes, and a velvet hood –
A present from the Gentlemen, along o' being good!
       Five and twenty ponies,
       Trotting through the dark –
       Brandy for the Parson,
       'Baccy for the Clerk.
Them that asks no questions isn't told a lie –
Watch the wall, my darling, while the Gentlemen go by!

Rudyard Kipling

The Wages of Sin

We're off to the hanging!
Our friends will be there,
With ribbons to wave
And a spyglass to share.

We're off to the hanging!
The crowd presses in,
It's good to be taught
The wages of sin.

We're off to the hanging!
The gibbet looms tall,
Somebody shouts
And the crowd starts to call.

We're off to the hanging!
A highwayman stands
Like a sorrowful prince
With a rose in his hand.

We're off to the hanging!
The crowd howls and shrieks,
The highwayman bows
And with dignity, speaks.

We're off to the hanging!
The crowd holds its breath,
The noose is a snake
That whispers of death.

We're off to the hanging!
The crowd roars and cheers,
I turn to the wall,
I cover my ears.

We're off to the hanging!
The highwayman swings,
While a terrible bell
In my head slowly rings.

We're back from the hanging!
But the sinner who bowed
Was finer by far
Than the murderous crowd.

Clare Bevan

The Field of Waterloo

Yea, the coneys are scared by the thud of hoofs,
And their white scuts flash at their vanishing heels,
And swallows abandon the hamlet-roofs.

The mole's tunnelled chambers are crushed by wheels,
The lark's eggs scattered, their owners fled;
And the hedgehog's household the sapper unseals.

The snail draws in at the terrible tread,
But in vain; he is crushed by the felloe-rim;
The worm asks what can be overhead,

And wriggles deep from a scene so grim,
And guesses him safe; for he does not know
What a foul red flood will be soaking him!

Beaten about by the heel and toe
Are butterflies, sick of the day's long rheum,
To die of a worse than the weather-foe.

Trodden and bruised to a miry tomb
Are ears that have greened but will never be gold,
And flowers in the bud that will never bloom.

Thomas Hardy

*The Battle of Waterloo took place on 18 June, 1815, and was the
battle where the Duke of Wellington's English Army defeated the
French emperor, Napoleon.*

Grace

It is no night for journeys.
Winds whine their way into a steady roar,
claw bellyfuls of ocean
into watery walls before us.
Dizzily we rise,
plunge into troughs below,
rise again, grip oars
and grasp for breath.
Cloud glowers all around,
dragged down to melt in spray;
beneath, the waiting ocean lies,
demanding, ever-hungry,
dark as death.

It is no night for journeys
yet ... somehow the boat,
enfolded like a wayward child
by loving, unseen arms,
holds fast beneath the starless night.
Between the thunder-roll of waves
and lashing sea-salt blurring sight
we hold our course,
believing only in
a safe return to light.

It was no night for journeys.

Judith Nicholls

*Grace Darling lived on the Farne Islands off the coast of Northumberland,
where her father was keeper of the Longstone Light. In 1838 she and her
father launched a small rowing boat in a fierce storm and rescued many
people from the paddle-steamer, the Forfarshire, which had been shipwrecked
on rocks nearby. Grace became a national heroine.*

Song for the Scullery Girl

Tie up your plaits;
Watch out for rats
When you go down to brush the mats.

Black the grate;
Don't be late;
Fetch the logs and lay them straight.

Start the fire;
Poke it higher,
Hang the brush back on the wire.

Mind you're quick
Don't miss a trick
If you're hanging about to flirt with Nick.

He's got no fears,
But if she hears
Cook will come and box *your* ears!

Then how you'll cry
And Nick might try
To chat up Susan by and by!

Make daily prayers
To Him who cares
And work your hardest Below Stairs.

Be it all your reward
To please your Lord
For that's where Heavenly treasures are stored.

Lyn Gregory

The Charge of the Light Brigade

Half a league, half a league,
Half a league onward,
All in the valley of Death
Rode the six hundred.
'Forward, the Light Brigade!
Charge for the guns!' he said:
Into the valley of Death
Rode the six hundred.

'Forward, the Light Brigade!'
Was there a man dismay'd?
Not tho' the soldier knew
Someone had blunder'd:
Their's not to make reply,
Their's not to reason why,
Their's but to do and die:
Into the valley of Death
Rode the six hundred.

Cannon to right of them,
Cannon to left of them,
Cannon in front of them
Volley'd and thunder'd;
Storm'd at with shot and shell,
Boldly they rode and well,
Into the jaws of Death,
Into the mouth of Hell
Rode the six hundred.

Flash'd all their sabres bare,
Flash'd as they turn'd in air
Sabring the gunners there,
Charging an army, while
All the world wonder'd:
Plunged in the battery-smoke
Right thro' the line they broke;
Cossack and Russian
Reel'd from the sabre-stroke
Shatter'd and sunder'd.
Then they rode back, but not
Not the six hundred.
Cannon to right of them,
Cannon to left of them;
Cannon behind them
Volley'd and thunder'd;
Storm'd at with shot and shell,
While horse and hero fell,
They that had fought so well
Came thro' the jaws of Death,
Back from the mouth of Hell,
All that was left of them.
Left of six hundred.

When can their glory fade?
O the wild charge they made!
All the world wonder'd.
Honour the charge they made!
Honour the Light Brigade,
Noble six hundred!

Alfred, Lord Tennyson

This poem was written about a fatal mistake in the Crimean War against Russia (1854–56), when British horse soldiers were ordered to charge the Russian guns in what proved to be a suicidal attempt to overpower them.

Climbing Boy

Ben climbed inside the chimneys
told to clean out all the soot,
    and those flues were black
    as a warlock's hat
and precarious underfoot.

A waif picked from the workhouse,
being five years old, and scared.
    He was light and slight
    as a widow's mite.
He knew nothing. No one cared.

At first afraid to clamber,
then his master lit some straw
    in the grate below
    so that Ben would know
the fear of burning more.

He scaled the crooked tunnels
with his brush, just sweeping blind.
So by slow degrees,
with his battered knees,
he became at last resigned.

At dawn he ate his gruel
and at night his loaf of bread.
Daily sixteen hours
in those nightmare towers
he just swept and cried and bled.

A grimy, ragged urchin,
he was one of many then.
Countless half-pint slaves
went to paupers' graves
too soon, brushed off, like Ben.

Jenny Morris

The Collar

I have to wear the collar
And stand here in the corner
And listen
While the teacher says that I'm a donkey.

A stupid Welsh donkey
Braying in a language
That marks me as a fool.
In school we mustn't speak
The language of heaven
Only English is acceptable.

But I forgot
And when he asked
The question
I answered
And the words leapt up
from my heart into my mouth
Wrong
All wrong

So I have to wear the collar
And hear how I'm a donkey
Until I learn
Until we all learn
Until we give up who we are
And everyone's like them.

Jan Dean

*In Victorian times children in Wales were forbidden to speak
Welsh in school. All things English were believed to be the highest
form of civilisation. Destroying Welsh was seen as progress, but
the Welsh call their language* 'yr iaith y nefoedd', *which means
'the language of heaven.'*

97

Victorian School Rhymes

You will never be sorry
For using gentle words,
For doing your best,
For being kind to the poor,
For looking before leaping,
For thinking before speaking,
For doing what you can to make others happy.

Anonymous

Why do drill?
Children who do drill,
Seldom are ill,
Seldom look pale,
Delicate and frail,
Seldom are sulky and
Seldom are spiteful
But always delightful.
So dears, I still
Beg you to drill.

Jennet Humphrey

Marching Rhyme

We march to our places,
With clean hands and faces,
And pay great attention
To all we are told.
For we know we shall never
Be happy and clever,
But learning is better
than silver and gold.

Anonymous

Preparing for Sunday

Haste! Put your playthings all away,
Tomorrow is the Sabbath Day.
Come bring o me your Noah's Ark,
Your pretty tinkling music cart:
Because my love, you must not play,
But holy keep the Sabbath Day.

Anonymous

Child Labour

'For oh,' say the children, 'we are weary
And we cannot run or leap;
If we care for any meadows, it were merely
To drop down in them and sleep.
Our knees tremble sorely in the stooping,
We fall upon our faces, trying to go;
And underneath our heavy eyelids drooping
The reddest flower would look as pale as snow.
For, all day, we drag our burden tiring
Through the coal-dark, underground;
Or, all day, we drive the wheels of iron
In the factories, round and round.

For all day the wheels are droning, turning;
Their wind comes in our faces,
Till our hearts turn, our heads with pulses burning,
And the walls turn in their places:
Turns the long light that drops adown the wall,
Turn the black flies that crawl along the ceiling:
All are turning, all the day, and we with all.
And all day, the iron wheels are droning,
And sometimes we could pray,
"O ye wheels" (breaking out in mad moaning)
"Stop! Be silent for today!"'

Elizabeth Barrett Browning

Nailers

Twelve blows
with the hammer.
One for each year.
He's twelve years old
as far as he knows.

Twelve blows
with the hammer
to make just one nail.
A thousand a day
to earn any pay.

Five pennies,
three farthings,
is all that's to show
for the pound of the hammer.

Brothers and sisters
who should be at school
to live and to learn
instead have to earn

a meagre living.
A poor, scanty meal
with the tools
that they know.

Hammers and nails.
Blow upon blow.

Ann Bonner

*Nail-making families were very poor. Children were taken
from school when they were ten to work in the trade.*

A Full Day in the Life of a King

Edward 7 woke up with a busy day ahead starting as
usual with breakfast including
*poached eggs haddock bacon mushrooms kidneys
chicken raspberries*

Followed by a fine morning shooting *pheasant woodcock
grouse duck ptarmigan*
as usual

Followed by returning for lunch with twelve courses
as usual including
*soup quail whiting grouse woodcock ptarmigan partridge
trout truffles sorbets*

Followed by racing at Ascot closely pursued by *tea with
pâté and crumpets*

Followed by the opera at Covent Garden including
from 8.30 to 9.30
interval refreshments prepared by six footmen with
tablecloths silver and gold plate
and a dozen hampers containing ten cold courses
consisting of as usual
*consommé lobster sole duck leveret lamb plovers'
eggs pigeon chicken
tongue and ham jelly oysters sandwiches desserts
patisseries*

Followed by Acts 4 and 5 and the applause
and the curtain coming down at last and the
                    royal coach leaving
with His Royal Highness Edward 7
containing His Royal Highness's royal interior
containing a large selection of *trout toast woodcock*
                    lobster patisseries plovers' eggs
bacon oysters pheasant haddock duck sorbets solos
                    duets cigar-smoke champagne

All shaken up together in the royal interior in the
                    royal coach
swaying slowly back to the palace

Where the king went to sleep with a small plate of
                    sandwiches by the bed
in case he got hungry as usual during the night

And so another full day came to an end
followed by next morning when Edward 7 woke up as
                    usual with a busy day ahead.

   Robert Hull

S.S. Titanic, 15th April, 1912

First was the silence. Not below,
where silver forks and laughter
chink in each saloon;
where layered decks of dance and song
echo through perfumed corridors,
all set to last till dawn.
Nor several tiers down
in simpler quarters.
There, for the first time ocean-borne,
emigrants still chatter,
more subdued in tone;
entrust to some far-off new world
their dreams
and all they own.

But high above the deck
is peace.
The wind is slight,
though air has chilled surprisingly:
little swell,
no waves to speak of,
movement smooth, unhampered.
The theatre set.
Viewed from the gods her course is clear,
pulled, as if by chains, on steady track
towards her destination.

Behind, the wake spreads endlessly,
stretches wide then slowly fades
into the night.

Only a faint jarring interrupts
that almost total silence of the sea,
barely noticed by the revellers.
There is no panic.
A brief encounter with an icy shelf
means nothing to a ship that is
unsinkable...

Later, she begins to list;
The rest is known.
Emigrants from flooded cabins
claw through dark companionways,
held back to save the rich;
lifeboats lowered quarter-full;
the shameless fights for precedence.

And for the rest,
gathering in disbelief on darkened decks,
the wait.
One weeps,
one lights a cigarette,
one goes below, changes to evening dress

to meet his fate.
On sloping decks the band play on –
Hold me up in high waters
their almost final line.

At last, she rises almost vertical –
a lifelong memory
for those who lived to tell the tale –
then slides, nose-first
towards her brave new world
encompassed only by
the lasting silence of the sea,
the silence of the sky.

Judith Nicholls

The Titanic *was considered 'unsinkable' when she was built. However, on her maiden voyage in April 1912, the ship hit an iceberg and sank. Over 1,500 lives were lost because the ship did not have enough lifeboats to save everyone on board.*

Walter William Henry Waines 1893–1916

Walter William Henry Waines
lost on the Somme.
No other names
appear upon
his cold, grey stone.
The family left behind?
Unknown.

Somewhere a wife,
somewhere a son,
a daughter
waiting,
soldiering on
like all those Lizzies, Harrys, Janes
who'd lost, to war, *their* Walter Waines.

Gina Douthwaite

Does it Matter?

Does it matter – losing your legs? ...
For people will always be kind,
And you need not show that you mind
When the others come in after hunting
To gobble their muffins and eggs.

Does it matter – losing your sight? ...
There's such splendid work for the blind;
And people will always be kind,
As you sit on the terrace remembering
And turning your face to the light.

Do they matter – those dreams from the pit? ...
You can drink and forget and be glad,
And people won't say that you're mad;
For they'll know that you've fought for your country,
And not one will worry a bit.

Siegfried Sassoon

In Flanders Fields

In Flanders fields the poppies blow
Between the crosses, row on row,
  That mark our place; and in the sky
  The larks, still bravely singing, fly
Scarce heard amid the guns below.

We are the Dead. Short days ago
We lived, felt dawn, saw sunset glow,
  Loved and were loved, and now we lie
      In Flanders fields.

Take up our quarrel with the foe:
To you from failing hands we throw
  The torch; be yours to hold it high.
  If ye break faith with us who die
We shall not sleep, though poppies grow
      In Flanders fields.

John McCrae

The Send-off

Down the close, darkening lanes they sang their way
To the siding shed,
And lined the train with faces grimly gay.

Their breasts were stuck all white with wreath and spray
As men's are, dead.

Dull porters watched them, and a casual tramp
Stood staring hard,
Sorry to miss them from the upland camp.
Then, unmoved, signals nodded, and a lamp
Winked to the guard.

So secretly, like wrongs hushed-up, they went.
They were not ours:
We never heard to which front these were sent.

Nor there if they yet mock what women meant
Who gave them flowers.

Shall they return to beatings of great bells
In wild train-loads?
A few, a few, too few for drums and yells,
May creep back, silent, to still village wells
Up half-known roads.

Wilfred Owen

*At the start of the First World War (1914–1918), soldiers were
cheered and bands played as they went off to France to fight.
Towards the end of the war, after so many soldiers had been
killed, everyone felt that there was no hope for the fresh troops
who seemed to be simply going to France to be slaughtered.*

'Do you remember 1926?'

Do you remember 1926? That summer of soups and
    speeches,
The sunlight on the idle wheels and the deserted crossings,
And the laughter and the cursing in the moonlit streets?
Do you remember 1926? The slogans and the penny concerts,
The jazz-bands and the moorland picnics,
And the slanderous tongues of famous cities?
Do you remember 1926? The great dream and the swift
    disaster,
The fanatic and the traitor, and more than all,
The bravery of the simple, faithful folk?
'Ay, ay, we remember 1926,' said Dai and Shinkin,
As they stood on the kerb in Charing Cross Road,
'And we shall remember 1926 until our blood is dry.'

Idris Davies

*1926 was the year of the General Strike. It lasted nine days
(3–12 May), beginning with a miner's strike and then extending
to a national stoppage of work by the transport industries,
building and printing trades, gas and electricity workers and
others. Many were victimised for having taken part in the action,
and there was widespread anger at the government's failure to
settle the miners' strike, which went on for another six months.*

Bournemouth,
September 3rd, 1939

My summer ends, and term begins next week.
Why am I here in Bournemouth, with my aunt
And 'Uncle Bill', who something tells me can't
Be really my uncle? People speak
In hushed, excited tones. Down on the beach
An aeroplane comes in low over the sea
And there's a scattering as people reach
For towels and picnic gear and books, and flee
Towards the esplanade. Back at the hotel
We hear what the Prime Minister has said.
'So it's begun.' 'Yes, it was bound to.' 'Well,
Give it till Christmas.' Later, tucked in bed,
I hear the safe sea roll and wipe away
The castles I had built in sand that day.

Anthony Thwaite

*3 September, 1939, was the date when England declared war on
Germany. It marked the start of the Second World War.*

Waiting To Be Met
(An Evacuee, 1940)

A child, too big to cry
I'd grown up in that year of war,
'was old enough' they said
to travel far, loneliness, a familiar friend,
came with me. The guard had helped me
to descend, unloading bag with me, clutching
my gas mask in its cardboard box, the pocket game.
He'd asked, in his country drawl
'You know her name?'
He meant the woman coming to collect me.
No one came.

The silence was immense
after the train had gone
late sunlight daubed the wooden seat,
the picket fence, against which I leant
too big to cry, and waited.
No one came.

I thought I heard a clock chime five
tolling into emptiness and fear;
then footsteps hurrying near, and through the gate
the woman came, unsmiling,
to take me to her home.
I stayed two years, but even now,
it seems upon reflection, that
no one ever came at Trowbridge Station.

Doris Corti

I've Finished
My Black-out
(The Song of a
Triumphant Housewife)

I've finished my Black-out!
    There's paint on the carpet and glue on my hair
    There's a saw in the bathroom and spills on the stair,
    And a drawing pin lost in the seat of a chair,
        But I've finished my Black-out.

The bedrooms are draped with funereal black
Except for the little one facing the back,
And that we have had to nail up with a sack,
        But I've finished my Black-out!

        Oh, I've finished my Black-out!
Policemen and wardens may peer and may pry,
And enemy planes may look down from the sky,
But they won't see a pin-prick however they try,
        For I've finished my Black-out!

Anonymous

*Once the Second World War started it was announced that all
lights had to be blacked-out so that German bombers would be
unable to spot targets from the air.*

Salvage Song
(or The Housewife's Dream)

My saucepans have all been surrendered,
The teapot is gone from the hob,
The colander's leaving the cabbage
For a very much different job.
So now, when I hear on the wireless
Of Hurricanes showing their mettle,
I see, in a vision before me,
A Dornier chased by my kettle.

Elsie Cawser

*To help with the war effort, Lord Beaverbrook made the
following appeal to the women of Britain: 'Give us your
aluminium and we will turn your pots and pans into Spitfires
and Hurricanes, Blenheims and Wellingtons.'*

*A Dornier is a German
bomber-plane*

Dunkirk (An extract)

All through the night, and in the next day's light
The endless columns came. Here was Defeat.
The men marched doggedly, and kept their arms,
But sleep weighed on their backs so that they reeled,
Staggering as they passed. Their force was spent.
Only, like old Horatius, each man saw
Far off his home, and seeing, plodded on.
At last they ceased. The sun shone down, and we
Were left to watch along a dusty road.

That night we blew our guns. We placed a shell
Fuze downwards in each muzzle. Then we put
Another in the breech, secured a wire
Fast to the firing lever, crouched, and pulled.
It sounded like a cry of agony,
The crash and clang of splitting, tempered steel.
Thus did our guns, our treasured colours, pass;
And we were left bewildered, weaponless,
And rose and marched, our faces to the sea.

We formed a line beside the water's edge.
The little waves made oddly home-like sounds,
Breaking in half-seen surf upon the strand.
The night was full of noise; the whistling thud
The shells made in the sand, and pattering stones;
The cries cut short, the shouts of unit's names;
The crack of distant shots, and bren gun fire;
The sudden clattering crash of masonry,
Steadily, all the time, the marching tramp
Of feet passed by along the shell-torn road,
Under the growling thunder of the guns.

The major said, 'The boats cannot get in,
'There is no depth of water. Follow me.'
And so we followed, wading in our ranks
Into the blackness of the sea. And there,
Lit by the burning oil across the swell,
We stood and waited for the unseen boats.

Oars in the darkness, rowlocks, shadowy shapes
Of boats that searched. We heard a seaman's hail.
Then we swam out, and struggled with our gear,
Clutching the looming gunwales. Strong hands pulled,
And we were in and heaving with the rest,
Until at last they turned. The dark oars dipped,
The laden craft crept slowly out to sea,
To where in silence lay the English ships.

B.G. Bonallack   May / June 1940

'Nothing, I feel, could be more English than the Battle of
Dunkirk, both in its beginning and its end, its folly and its
grandeur.'
J.B. Priestly's Postscript, 5 June 1940

*In June 1940 the British army fighting in France were driven back
by German forces until they reached the coast at Dunkirk.
Thousands of troops were massed upon the beaches. They were
successfully rescued by a flotilla of little ships that sailed across
the Channel from England and helped to ferry the soldiers to
bigger ships that waited in deeper water.*

Picture from the Blitz

After all these years
I can still close my eyes and see
her sitting there,
in her big armchair,
grotesque under an open sky,
framed by the jagged lines of her broken house.

Sitting there,
a plump homely person,
steel needles still in her work-rough hands;
grey with dust, stiff with shock,
but breathing,
no blood or distorted limbs;
breathing, but stiff with shock,
knitting unravelling on her apron'd knee.

They have taken the stretchers off my car
and I am running
under the pattering flack
over a mangled garden;
treading on something soft
and fighting the rising nausea –
only a far-flung cushion, bleeding feathers.

They lift her gently
out of her great armchair,
tenderly,
under the open sky,
a shock-frozen woman trailing khaki wool.

Lois Clark

*'The Blitz' was a phrase for the German bombing raids on British
cities in 1940 and 1941. The term comes from the German word
'blitzkrieg', meaning 'lightning war'.*

Underground

When creatures hear the hunter
They dive inside their holes,
And we hide under London
Like frightened, human moles.

Like frightened, human moles
We shudder in the dark
Below the starry city,
The palace and the park.

The palace and the park
Are shining bright as noon,
While hawks of death are swooping
Beneath a traitor moon.

Beneath a traitor moon
The bombers dive and drone,
We huddle in our tunnels
Each one of us alone.

Each one of us alone
Amongst the sweating crowd,
Too scared to plan tomorrow,
Too shy to pray out loud.

Too shy to pray out loud
As fear infects the mind...
When morning lifts her black-out
What horrors will we find?

What horrors will we find,
What savage, smoking holes?
We who creep from darkness
Like frightened, human moles.

Clare Bevan

When London was being bombed night after night during the Blitz, the government ordered that the Underground should be left open once the trains had finished running so that people could shelter there.

Hiroshima

Noon, and hazy heat;
A single silver and a dull drone;
The gloved finger poised, pressed:
A second's silence, and
Oblivion.

Anonymous

*The war against Japan ended soon after the dropping of
atomic bombs on the cities of Hiroshima and Nagasaki.*

1945

The news was of inhumanity,
Of crimes, obscenities,
Unspeakable insanity
And bestial atrocities.

Somebody turned the radio down.
Nobody said a word.
Auschwitz, Buchenwald, and Belsen:
'It couldn't happen here,' they said.

At school the teacher set revision:
Of the princes murdered in the tower,
The Spanish Inquisition,
And Ghengis Khan drunk with power;

Of heretics, burnt at the stake,
Refusing to deny a vow;
Mass-murders for religion's sake;
He said, 'It couldn't happen now.'

'You're next,' the school-bullies snigger,
'Don't try any silly tricks!'
All through History he tries to figure
A way out of punches and kicks.

At the end of morning-school,
They drag him to an air-raid shelter.
Down into darkness, damp and cool,
With Puncher and Kicker and Belter.

They tear off all his clothes
And tread them on the floor.
With obscenities and oaths,
They let him have what-for.

Their tortures are very crude,
Clumsy and unrefined.
With a sudden change of mood
They pretend to be friendly and kind.

They change their tack once more
And punch him black and blue.
He ends, crouched on the floor,
And finally they're through.

With a special parting kick
They warn him not to talk.
He feels wretched, sore and sick,
Gets up, can hardly walk.

It's a beautiful Summer day,
His eyes squint in the sun.
He hears two passing women say,
'Oh, schooldays are such fun.'

Words echo in his head:
'Couldn't happen here,' they said.
And 'Couldn't happen now,' they said.
He never breathes a word.

Geoffrey Summerfield

Street Party

Out came the tables, the chairs and the plates,
the hard-bristled brooms and the buckets, too.
The whole street was swept from end to end
by grannies and grandads and grandchildren, too.
Out from the back of the larder's store,
Came packets and tins which had been hoarded for
just such an occasion as this.
On new scrubbed tables the cakes and jellies,
crowd in beside the rolls and the buns,
paper hats and crackers with cheap silly mottoes,
add to feeling that street parties are fun.
Old Mrs Hyacinth, who's ninety-four,
muttered that she seen it all before.
She can remember – and she does at length –
the battles and tales of the Boer War.
Peace comes and it goes, and she says she knows,
Since she's been to these parties so often before.
She mutters crossly through zippered teeth,
'Stop all this talking and let's eat.'

Brown Betty teapots, in bright wollen hats,
Fill mugs and beakers and bone china cups
Right to the brim with black, tarry tea.
Sandwiches and squash complete this spread.
From upstairs windows, Union Jacks
Flutter and stir in the afternoon breeze.
Then someone starts singing, 'God Save the King.'
Soon nights starts to fall, but no one goes home.
Harry Gillespie, from number fourteen,
fetches his fiddle and begins to play
Waltzes and tangoes and everyone dances,
Laughing and chattering till dawn breaks the next day.

Janis Priestley

*The end of the Second World War (1945) was celebrated with
many street parties.*

Did You Know?

Did you know you could:–
Run a car with a gas balloon
Make omelettes with powder
Play houses under a table
Go without sweets
Light a room with gas
Wash with a cold tap
Keep warm with a shovel full of coal
Have kippers as a treat
Not know what a banana was?
Most people had:–
No cars
Varnished floors and lino
No fridges
No bathrooms
No central heating
No television
Did you know:–
There were British Restaurants (sugar spoons chained to
    the counters).
No MacDonalds!
There was Woolton Pie, Snook, whalemeat but not Burgers.
Vegetables were home grown, life wriggled happily in each
    leaf fold.
You washed clothes with Rinso, Persil and great green
    squares of Fairy Soap.
Soda stripped the hands raw when meal-time washing up
    was done.

Radios were bakelite with great glass valves inside them.
Battery run, water filled, we heaved them from the
refilling shop.
People used buses with a conductor and a driver.
Trains ran on steam dirtying hands and filling eyes
with cinders.
Toys made with celluloid, not plastics yet, caught fire easily
with a spark from Dad's Woodbine.
Whips and tops, cowboys and indians, playground chants
filled the time.
We grouped as gangs, not playing alone with electronic toys.
Crisps had blue bags of salt in them.
Sucking them happily we drank gallons of Tizer.
Most old people say:–
Those were the good old days.
WHAT DO YOU THINK?

Karlen Lawrence

Mum, Dad and Me

My parents grew among palmtrees,
in sunshine strong and clear.
I grow in weather that's pale,
misty, watery or plain cold,
around back streets of London.

Dad swam in warm sea, at my age.
I swim in a roofed pool.
Mum – she still doesn't swim.

Mum went to an open village market
at my age. I go to a covered
arcade one with her now.
Dad works most Saturdays.

At my age Dad played
cricket with friends.
Mum helped her mum, or talked
shouting halfway up a hill.
Now I read or talk on the phone.

With her friends Mum's mum washed
clothes on a river-stone. Now
washing-machine washes our clothes.
We save time to eat to TV,
never speaking.

My dad longed for a freedom in Jamaica.
I want a greater freedom.
Mum prays for us, always.

Mum goes to church
some evenings and Sundays.
I go to the library.
Dad goes for his darts at the local.

Mum walked everywhere, at my age.
Dad rode a donkey.
Now I take a bus
or catch the underground train.

James Berry

*In the 1950s, Britain started to become
a multi-cultural society. People from
Caribbean countries were
encouraged to emigrate
to Britain and work.*

History Lesson

My aunty says
She remembers when the first sputnik,
Like a spiky yo-yo
Circled around the world
Singing its mournful beep, beep, beep.
Her father was so excited
He danced on the rug shouting,
'Miracles! History!
Listen to this.'
But she was reading her Superman comic
And laughed at the fuss.

My dad says
He remembers that first trip to the moon,
Fuzzy men in fat suits
Wading through dust to plant their limp flags
And call their crackled messages.
His teacher was so excited
She danced around the classroom crying,
'Miracles! History!
Listen to this!'
But the children were too busy making alien masks
For the school play
And smiled at the fuss.

Today, my teacher tells me to watch the news.
Robot voyagers probe the red mysteries of Mars,
Trundle their wide wheels under the
Astonished stars.
The reporter dances in his seat saying,
'Miracles! History!
Listen to this.'
But I prefer the space cartoons
With their shiny, silver villains,
And I yawn at the fuss.

When my turn comes to cry,
'Listen to this!'
I hope there will still be some miracles to see
And a little bit of history
Left for me.

Clare Bevan

Missiles in Cuba

I was twelve years old
when Kennedy muscled up to Khruschev
over missiles in Cuba,
when Cold War bluff and counter-bluff
took the world to the brink.
I learnt a new word –
Armaggedon –
'It could happen here,'
the papers proclaimed,
'It could happen now.'

I questioned my parents constantly,
were we all about to die?
My father, grim faced,
spoke only of the last lot,
of how they survived.
But the world had rolled on since then,
more fuses, more fire power.
My eyes pleaded with him,
say it will be OK.
But he was frightened, too,
I could tell.

We tiptoed about the house,
it didn't seem right to play Elvis songs,
no 'Good Luck Charm' would stop this war,
I knew the score on that one.
And why should I worry about tests at school,
we could all be blown to pieces
come the weekend.

My father said it was prayer that was needed,
but prayer wasn't doing any good.

And I remember that last chance Sunday,
all of us praying in church,
praying so hard it hurt,
then coming back home to find
they'd backed away,
stepped down from the abyss.

Out in the garden I stood beneath the stars,
breathed in,
breathed deep,
breathed a future.

Brian Moses

*In October 1962 America realised that Russian missile launching
sites were being constructed on the Communist island of Cuba,
only 90 miles from the coast of America. President Kennedy sent
warnings to Khruschev, the Russian President, that this would not
be tolerated. America then set up a naval blockade or
'quarantine' area around Cuba to prevent the sites from being
completed. This brought these two super powers to the brink of
nuclear war, and for six days the world held its breath...*

Terrorist's Wife

A phone-call takes him
into the darkness for weeks.
In the mornings, his absence
fills me with dread. I thin my eyes
to watch for cars that come to wait
down in the street. All day
I move from room to room. I polish
each spotless place
to a chill shining. Fear tracks me
like hunger. In the silence,
the walls grow water-thin.
The neighbours wear masks –
tight lips, veiled looks, such
fine tissues of knowing.
My mother doesn't visit. I drag
my shopping from the next town.

Once, putting his clean shirts away,
my dry hands touched a shape
that lay cold and hard. I wept then,
and walked for hours in the park.
I listened for his name in the news.
When I looked at our sleeping son
my sadness thickened.
His comings are like his goings –
a swift movement in the night.

At times, he can sit here for days
meticulously groomed; primed,
watching soccer games on TV,
our child playful on his lap.
But scratch the smooth surface
of his mood, and how
the breached defences spit their fire.

Now, when he holds me to him,
I know I taste murder
on his mouth. And in the darkness,
when he turns from me, I watch him
light a cigarette. In his palm
the lighter clicks and flames.
Balanced, incendiary.

Angela Greene

*In 1969 the British
army was sent to
Northern Ireland to
keep order. The IRA
(Irish Republican Army)
began a terrorist
campaign to force
the British soldiers
to leave.*

Peace Process

Things are finally moving,
a spokesperson says.

Even now officials
are on their knees measuring

the huge handshake
the leaders did up there,

while specialists scrutinise
the innards of smiles.

It appears the leaders
may have been alone long enough

to consummate a sentence,
which could mean that the people

may yet be permitted
not to run out of future.

Robert Hull

Index of Authors

Acknowledgements

The compiler and publishers gratefully acknowledge permission to reproduce the following copyright material:

Barbara Levy Literary Agency for Siegfried Sassoon's *Does It Matter?* copyright © Siegfried Sassoon by kind permission of George Sassoon;

Clare Bevan for *The Priest Hole, The Wages of Sin, History Lesson, Underground* and *Cardinal Wolsey*;

Ann Bonner for *Nailers*, copyright © Ann Bonner 2004;

Curtis Brown Group Ltd for Anthony Thwaite's *Bournemouth, September 3rd 1939*, reproduced with permission of Curtis Brown Group Ltd, London on behalf of Anthony Thwaite, copyright © Anthony Thwaite;

Dave Calder for *Bess's Bath*;

Carcanet Press Limited for Vicki Raymond's *Beaker Burial* in 'Selected Poems';

Alison Chisholm for *Sea Dreaming, Grape Lane* and *Place of the Plague Wife;*

Doris Corti for *Waiting to be Met*;

Charles Causley for *Lady Jane Grey;*

Jan Dean for *The Collar* and *Question Asked at the Yorvik Centre*;

Gina Douthwaite for *Walter William Henry Waines;*

Faber and Faber Limited for W H Auden's *Roman Wall Blues from Collected Shorter Poems* (Faber and Faber Limited);

Gomer Press Ltd for Idris Davies' *Do You Remember 1926?*

Mary Green for *My Extraordinary Life;*

Lyn Gregory for *Song for the Scullery Girl, Stowaway* and *Last Wife;*

Gus Grenfell for *Battle of Falkirk 1298*;

David Harmer for *They Shall Receive a Great Blow* and *At Senlac Hill;*

Trevor Harvey for *To See or Not To See*;

Stewart Henderson for *King Robert the Bruce: The Spider Replies* from the collection 'All things Weird and Wonderful' by Stewart Henderson published by Lion Children's Books © 2003;

David Higham Associates Limited for Eleanor & Herbert Farjeon's *Oliver Cromwell* and *James I* in 'Kings and Queens' (Jane Nissen Books);

Jason Hulme for *Amphitheatre at Deva*;

Mike Johnson for *Roman Baths*;

Jean Kenward for *The Flint;*

Daphne Kitching for *Night Thoughts of Oliver Cromwell*;

Ian Larmont for *Bosworth Field*;

Patricia Leighton for *Silent Stones* and *A Viking Prays to His Gods*;

Rowena M. Love for *Fireships;*

Brian Moses for *The Children of Witches*, *Missiles in Cuba* and *Love Letter From Mary Tudor to Her Husband Philip of Spain;*

Judith Nicholls for *SS Titanic* © Judith Nicholls 1994, from 'Storm's Eye' by Judith Nicholls, pub. Oxford University Press. Reprinted by permission of the author; and for *Grace* © Judith Nicholls 2003, reprinted by permission of the author;

Penguin Books Ltd for Benjamin Zephaniah's *The Celts,* from 'Wicked World' by Benjamin Zephaniah (Puffin, 2000), copyright © Benjamin Zephaniah, 2000;

PFD for Robert Hull's *Peace Process* and *A Full Day in the Life of a King*, reprinted by permission of The Peters Fraser and Dunlop Group Limited on behalf of Robert Hull © Robert Hull; and for James Berry's *Mum, Dad and Me*, on behalf of James Berry © James Berry;

Jim Pointon for *Bitter Winds*;

Peggy Poole for *Home Coming 1648*;

Joan Poulson for *Encourage the Oxen* and *Tod Boucher*;

Janis Priestly for *Street Party*;

Rogers, Coleridge & White Ltd for Kevin Crossley Holland's *Riddle No. 5 (The Shield)* and *Riddle No. 3 (Fire)*, copyright © Kevin Crossley Holland 1978 c/o Rogers, Coleridge and White Ltd, 20 Powis Mews, London W11 1JN;

Cynthia Rider for *The Fire of London 1666*;

Diane Schneider for *Screamasax*;

Matt Simpson for *Cry God for Harry;*

AP Watt Ltd on behalf of The Nationl Trust for Places of Historical Interest or Natural Beauty for Rudyard Kipling's *A Pict Song* and *A Smuggler's Song*.

About Brian Moses

Brian Moses lives on the Sussex coast with his wife and two daughters. He writes and edits poetry and picture books for young people. Brian travels extensively in both the UK and abroad, presenting his poetry and percussion shows in schools, libraries and at festivals. He has always had a strong interest in history and has written a number of historical titles for Hodder Wayland. His latest publications are *So You Want to Write Poetry* and *Poems Out Loud* (both published by Hodder Wayland).